Practical Topics in Correctional Education

Alisa Smedley

Minus2OPublications

Book Cover Design by Kimb Williams Graphic Design

Contents

Introduction

Practical Topics in Correctional Education Vol. I is a guide and workbook for correctional educators. My name is Coach Smedley and I have been on this correctional education road for many years. I am providing the information here so that other educators can discover or remember what they love about this field. Or not. My goal is to inform, inspire, coach, and equip you with the skills that you will need in order to be effective.

Let's begin with a reality check. It is important to fully understand where we are today. One half of our job is **education**. Education in general has become more complex over the years. We encounter students from various backgrounds and academic levels. Resources in some school districts are vanishing before our eyes. We will not even discuss the issue of adequate compensation for our hard work!

The other half of our job is **corrections**. Whether you physically work inside a jail, prison, transitional center, etc. or you work fully in the community, most of our learners have encountered some aspect of the criminal legal system. Understanding the corrections part of our job helps us to 1) navigate the work environment of corrections and 2) empathize with our students and the things they experience while incarcerated.

Basically, you work within two industries that are fraught with issues. I do not say this to discourage you. Rather, I want you to be informed. If you were hiking and became lost in the woods, your survival would depend on your knowledge of the terrain and survival skills that you possess. Our job is kind of like that. You will not survive the environment if you don't fully understand it. *Your journey will be unnecessarily difficult if you don't gain some basic information early on*. As a veteran educator I offer this information to promote maximum effectiveness on the job.

Full disclosure – I am by nature a pretty direct person. It is my opinion that we cannot afford to waste precious time being politically correct in our work. My super power in the classroom is my bluntness. In fact, I believe that bluntness is the new nurturing when dealing with students. They appreciate that Coach Smedley is real! I hope that you, too, will appreciate this gift of mine. The opinions and observations included in this guide are my own. Most are backed up by scientific evidence while others are simply my viewpoint. I will let you know when I am giving my opinion.

Practical Topics in Correctional Education Vol. I will focus on you, some typical work environments and conditions, and practical strategies to help you to survive and thrive. My follow-up tool is **Practical Topics in Correctional Education Vol. II** which turns the lens toward our students. Within those pages I provide you with wisdom and insight that will increase your shelf-life and improve student engagement.

I did not set out to write an academic treatment of our work. Rather, my goal is to provide you with a down to earth, practical guide that will elicit an occasional chuckle along the way. Correctional education is so serious! Let's enjoy this "hike" through the field as we examine our unique world together. Along the way I will share stories from the front line of correctional education from both me and several dear colleagues. I hope you enjoy the journey.

– Coach Smedley

How to Use This Guide

Practical Topics in Correctional Education Vol. I is designed to be informative, light reading for a tough job. You can read chapters in order, or you can select the chapter that interests you in the moment. Each chapter can be enjoyed as a stand alone essay. In each chapter you will find the following sections:

- *Introduction to the theme* – each chapter begins with a few words about the theme of the chapter.

- *The Main Point* – this chapter summary contains a few sentences that discuss the most important realities discussed in the chapter. If you are glancing through and want to pick a chapter to read, look at the Main Point for guidance.

- *My "AHA" moment* – is a detailed discussion using actual examples and experiences that are related to the chapter theme.

- *Professional Development Activity* – this section asks you to *apply* the information you learned in the chapter to build practical skills. Some exercises will provide an outlet for you to express things you may be feeling about the job.

- *Voices from the Field* – this section shares comments from veteran correctional educators from across the country related to the chapter theme.

- *Self-Care* – the final section of each chapter provides quick self-care suggestions for you to implement. Toxic, unstructured, poorly managed environments are a huge drain. The Self Care tips can help you to detox.

- *My Reflections on this Chapter* – this is your blank space to write down thoughts, ideas, and responses to what you read in the chapter.

1

What Makes a Good Correctional Educator?

You make a difference every single day. And you get to choose what sort of difference you want to make. Jane Goodall

This is a great question. As important as correctional educators are, we are not the most important position in corrections. I mean let's face it. The key staff in a correctional environment is the uniformed officer. They outnumber every other group – administration, support staff, medical staff, etc. The uniformed officer is extremely vital to the safety and protection of everyone who enters the building. This is why having the wrong uniformed staff leads to so many systemic problems including contraband, violence, and sexual misconduct. Let me say that most of the officers are true professionals. It is the occasional bad hire that I am referring to, and that can happen for any position within the agency or facility.

It is not my intention to begin with such a heavy topic. I mention this issue now because doing your job well requires your understanding of how you fit into the organization. It also helps if you can spot personality traits and behaviors that will make your job more difficult. Enough on that subject, Coach Smedley will stay in her lane.

As far as correctional educators are concerned, I can tell you without hesitation the traits that do NOT make for good correctional educators. This is not the job for certain personality types and behaviors. The short list of who not to be includes – childish, gossip, nosey, etc. Let's examine each of these types in the context of correctional education:

The Child – correctional education is serious business! A teacher who plays around too much is a liability in an environment where you are being watched by the incarcerated individuals. Childish behavior makes you gullible for manipulation, and an easy target for being "set-up." Be a grown up at all times, please.

The Gossip – a teacher who talks too much, especially about sensitive issues, is also a problem. Whether gossiping about fellow staff, incarcerated individuals, volunteers, or whomever, it is all dangerous. If you become known for spilling the tea, don't be surprised when everyone wants some! I can tell you from witnessing this dynamic many times, the gossip is always embroiled in messy situations. You must have discretion when it comes to the information that you will have access to.

The Nosey – the nosey teacher is a twin to "The Gossip." This teacher always wants to know information that has nothing to do with them. This personality type loves having knowledge and weaponizing it! As I have mentioned, you will be exposed to enough information in the course of a day that you don't need to go actively looking for more.

The Agitator – is the teacher who is always agitated, angry, yelling at every request when it is not necessary. They are dangerous in a correctional setting because they ignite others around them, especially inmates. They change the energy in every room that they walk in to. When you encounter the agitator, try to stay calm and steady. Do not let yourself get pulled into their frenzy.

The Friend – this teacher wants to make friends with everyone. They will try to appease staff or students. This personality type is a follower who desperately wants to be in the club. They pretend to care about everyone only to get in close. I certainly hope that you already have friends before starting the job! It is acceptable to be friendly and cordial. I would advise that you avoid getting too close at work.

The Seducer – this person is flirty, and overtly sexy. They enjoy being looked at by as many eyeballs as possible. They tend to dress far too sexy for the corrections environment. They send a message of availability that is dangerous. Most seducers typically do not cross the line, but they sure come too close for comfort. Bottom line, dress and carry yourself appropriately.

THE MAIN POINT

Certain personality types and behaviors make the job more dangerous! This is a job for mature, serious adults. Broken, insecure, and dysfunctional staff will cause trouble for themselves or others.

MY "AHA" MOMENT

I have worked with each of these types during my years in the field. You may not encounter each type, or you may encounter *different types*. I would just tell you to be on the lookout. And make sure that you are not becoming a type yourself!

The moment that really influenced how I carry myself happened one Fall. I will skip the details but share the important lesson that I learned. It all started with me making a mistake. It was a medium sized mistake, but I was in the "headlines" inside my facility. Being in the headlines happens when the whole building has heard about your screw up. Corrections has slow periods where not much is happening, and staff do a lot of standing or sitting and talking. Lots of talking!

When something juicy occurs, you are the headline news until the next big story. So, Coach Smedley spent a few weeks in the headlines. It was at this moment that I took a major professional step – I owned it. The fault for the mistake was not mine entirely, but as the senior staff in my area it became my mess. I acknowledged it, took my lumps and kept my head down in the aftermath. One the one hand keeping my head down kept me away from more drama. But I also needed to walk into the building with my head held high every day. Because I knew that I had to continue working for my other students. All the while knowing that I was being whispered about throughout the building. It was hard, but life went on. Nothing like that even remotely ever happened again.

The beauty of that experience is that my reputation survived. It became known that if something went wrong, and Coach Smedley was under scrutiny, she would face it head on. She would not try to hide a mistake, shift blame to someone else, or make excuses. During that time spent in the headlines, I realized that people made note of how I handled it. I earned respect during that period of time.

Three traits that I developed over the years have defined my career. They are **integrity**, **maturity**, and **professionalism**. I strongly suggest that you discover the type of correctional educator that you want to become. As you do so, consider your influence over your students, your team, your facility, and your industry at large. That is how you keep growing and identifying opportunities in your career. What traits would you like to be known for in your career? Write them in this space.

Professional Development Activity

For your first professional development activity think about the *types* that Coach Smedley talks about. List and describe the types you have encountered on the chart labeled *Dysfunctional Types in Correctional Education*. You may have new types that Coach Smedley did not mention, feel free to list and describe the behavior. On the chart labeled *My Observation Journal* discuss how you are impacted by these types.

Dysfunctional Types in Correctional Education

Types that I encounter at work and their behaviors

Type

Type

Type

Type

Dysfunctional Types in Correctional Education

MY OBSERVATIONS JOURNAL

DATE:

_____

_____

_____

_____

_____

_____

_____

_____

_____

_____

_____

_____

_____

_____

_____

_____

_____

_____

My Observations Journal

Voices from the Field

Coach Smedley encourages you to meet other correctional educators at conferences, collaborative projects, or PD training. You will hear from some of my network at the end of each chapter. My colleague Jolene works in Iowa. Her advice for being a good correctional educator is to *"lead by example by always keeping your word, apologizing when you make a mistake, being punctual and prepared for class. These are all real world behaviors we want our students to have so we must lead by example. Correctional education is an amazing career. I absolutely love what I do, and know that I am making a difference in my students' lives. I wish you all the best as you pursue this career opportunity. I hope you'll find years of satisfaction and success" – Jolene*

Self-Care Reminders

1. Pace yourself to avoid burn-out.

2. Find a professional network outside of your facility or agency.

3. Ask yourself the question – "Am I clear about my professional goals?"

My Chapter 1 Reflection

What are your **takeaways** from this chapter? What **action steps** will you take moving forward? Was there anything said that really hit home with you? Use this section after each chapter to brainstorm your ideas, thoughts, and feelings. Begin journaling anything about your current position that needs to be addressed. You can also look ahead and dream about the goals that you want to pursue. Let's go!

2

Customer Service & Correctional Education

Service is the rent that you pay for room on this earth. Shirley Chisolm

I get asked all of the time how I got into correctional education. As many of you know, there are various ways to get here. Perhaps you are a K-12 licensed teacher who is finding a second career in correctional education. Or you may be a criminal justice graduate who has a natural gift for explaining things and leading groups? Some people sign up to work with the incarcerated, while others are drafted. *"Hey counselor Jones, you can do reentry groups a few times a week can't you?"* Sound familiar?

Over the years, I have experienced working both *behind the wall* (code for working inside a carceral setting such as a jail or prison) and beyond the wall. I've worked inside maximum security facilities, halfway houses, and drug treatment centers. My employers ranged from non-profit agencies to government entities, to private ventures. Like I said, many roads lead to this work. I am sure that you, too, have an interesting story about finding your current job. How did you get here?

Regardless of how you got here, you may now find yourself working with second chance students/clients/customers. The language keeps changing, but the fundamental work remains the same. *Helping those who are justice impacted to reintegrate back into society while reducing recidivism*. That is what we do.

Whatever road got you here, I think that it is extremely important to approach the job with a spirit of good customer service. It makes sense to start the conversation with customer service. When you work in correctional education utilizing **transferable skills** from any past employment situations can increase your odds of success.

Why do I say this? Well, your training may be lopsided. Here are three scenarios to illustrate my point:

Scenario #1: You may be employed by a correctional facility and receive *correctional training* that includes swipe cards, tactical training, custody and security protocols, etc. but includes nothing about classroom management of incarcerated learners. How do you juggle educational goals while understanding custody and security matters?

Scenario #2: Your employer might be a community college partner. In this scenario you are immersed in the academic policies and procedures required for student success and then sent off to report to the correctional facility every day or a few days a week. You are totally unprepared for the correctional environment. You may have to rely on random peers who take pity on you and decide to teach you the ropes!

Scenario #3: In another scenario your employer is the local workforce development entity. You get certain correctional facility tools (email, equipment and office space, for example), but you are not technically part of the correctional facility or culture. You find yourself constantly in hot water for breaking unspoken rules that you did not even know about!

That is what I mean when I say that your training may be lopsided. You may be missing key components needed for you to do the job. When this happens, you are instantly in survival mode! And all you wanted to do was teach. Can you relate?

I have worked in all three of the scenarios described above. For years! These experiences caused extreme stress to me and my family. More than once I wanted to quit the profession all together. Fortunately, I learned survival skills that I will gladly share with you, which is one of my main reasons for writing this guide.

THE MAIN POINT

When you are thrown into a challenging position that you feel unprepared for, remember your past victories. Use transferable skills to show you the path to success on your current job.

MY "AHA" MOMENT

Three of my previous jobs prepared me for working in correctional education. My experiences from retail, park maintenance, and real estate provided me with valuable transferable skills. Looking back, I have come to under-stand that these transferable skills allowed me to do this work while maintaining a healthy and positive attitude. And I have not quit the profession...yet.

Retail

It is my belief that everyone needs to "serve time" working in retail. Working a retail job teaches you incredible stamina and patience. You also learn how to work under pressure. And the conditions are often undesirable - long hours, low wages, and demanding customers. You will sometimes be offered last minute, unexpected hours when your co-worker quits. You are also tasked with meeting customer requests that are beyond your control. And you may get yelled at despite your best effort! The more I think about it, retail was a lot like working in correctional education.

Park Maintenance

I spent a few summers during college working in park maintenance. My job was to clean the park after parties, festivals, rallies, protests, etc. I removed broken glass. Cleaned up wine bottles, cigarette butts, and at times some pretty mysterious substances. It took hours to pick up, toss out, and carry away literally pounds of trash! It was peaceful work, though. I walked a lot and restored the park to beauty and order. Actually, working that job was symbolic of the kind of work that I do now, only in a different way. Don't we help our students remove some nasty experiences and memories? Aren't we hoping to help them find beauty and meaning in their future lives after some not so pretty events?

Real Estate

The last job that helped to prepare me for correctional education was my twelve-year stint in real estate. I learned to overcome objections. I also had to help my customers deal with reality *("No, you can't buy THAT house, it is out of your price range!")*. Through the process of listening, educating, and even scolding, I watched my customers grow. Some stubbornly insisted on doing things their way and ignored my wisdom. Others were ungrateful. Occasionally, though, I truly helped some of my customers. The young couple that reached a dream that they thought was impossible. Or the aging homeowner who just wanted a fair price when selling the last home they would ever own. Real estate taught me to listen and to try to help people meet their needs or achieve their dreams. Even while gently helping them to accept certain realities.

I guess the bottom line is that these jobs all taught me about customer service. Even when my "customer" was a park. We will never fail in our jobs as correctional educators if we remember to deliver good customer service! Respect people. Work with them even when they are being unreasonable. Hear them. Care for them.

Do you understand now how accessing my transferable skills helped me to continue working in correctional education? I am reminded of who I am. The gifts that I bring to the table and the beautiful work of helping broken people or broken systems.

Professional Development Activity

Take a moment to think back to previous jobs that you have had. On the chart labeled *Transferable Skills Activity Step 1*, list the position and the main skills that you gained from three past jobs. On *Transferable Skills Activity Step 2*, think about ways that you can utilize skills that you identified in Step 1 in your current position. Also, think about new skills that you are going to need in order to be successful.

My Skills from Previous Jobs

Job #1

Job #2

Job #3

Transferable Skills Activity Step 1

Transferable Skills

Ways I Can Utilize These Skills Now

New Skills I Need to Learn

Transferable Skills Activity Step 2

Voices from the Field

Gwen provides a money management workshop at a community-based correctional center in Cleveland, Ohio. Her curriculum is designed specifically for correctional learners. Gwen says *"we have to go above and beyond in how we deliver our services and information. The people we serve could easily be our own sons or daughters, aunts or uncles. We can't save everybody, but we can SERVE as many as we possibly can if they are ready to hear our message."*

Self-Care Reminders

1. Get your proper rest and exercise.

2. Find a creative hobby to recharge your batteries.

3. Read, watch or listen to leading sales trainers from the world of business.

My Chapter 2 Reflection

3

Exploring Saturn

Everything that irritates us about others can lead us to an understanding of ourselves. Carl Gustav Jung

I decided to write about working inside correctional education because it is unlike any other work environment. Has anyone ever asked what you do for a living, and then followed up with *"How can I get into that?"* Probably not. If you are like me, most of the time people will tell you how they could NEVER do what you do! And guess what? I think they are right.

It takes a special person to walk into the places that we enter and do the work that we do. Our field demands competence, compassion, toughness, intelligence, and humor. WOW. What a combination of skills and personality traits. Yet each is necessary for our success. Can you think of other skills that are needed?

If I were to try to explain our world to outsiders, it would be difficult. Many people believe everything that they see on shows about prison life or riding with cops on the street. I rarely watch those because they are either wildly exaggerated or do not begin to capture the reality of what we see at work.

Let me say that I have the highest respect and admiration for our uniformed peers. Police officers who fight crime on the streets get a higher level of glory. People tend to forget the role of uniformed staff inside correctional environments. They are the authority figures who spend a lot more time with incarcerated individuals. Given the current national staffing crisis, uniformed officers practically live at their posts.

I thought of a creative way to try to explain or at least describe our work to lay people. I will ask them to imagine exploring Saturn. That's right, the huge 6th planet from the sun has a lot in common with our field and *is just as foreign to outsiders*. A few fun facts about Saturn along with my comparisons to corrections in bold:

Days on Saturn last approximately 10 hours. That means that the planet rotates on its axis while here on Earth it takes 24 hours to accomplish the same thing. **Days can pass at a dizzying pace**.

Saturn is huge! It is estimated that it would take nine Earths to match its diameter. **It is a large and complex system**.

The atmosphere of Saturn is gaseous, being made up of hydrogen and helium. **In other words, it's full of hot air.** (No comment)

Did you notice how I slipped some facts about Saturn into the discussion? That is how we can build our students' knowledge base, one little fact at a time. Seriously though, entering our world with the eyes of an explorer could be useful. Whether you are new to correctional education or have a few years under your belt, ride along with me as we examine the correctional ecosystem.

One of the first things that I noticed during new staff orientation is how many teams or "tribes" some institutions have. The leadership, the healthcare team, the counseling staff, clerical, kitchen, maintenance workers, and on and on. It takes an enormous team of people and various departments to adequately staff a correctional facility. That does not even include the vendors who provide everything from commissary to floormats to cleaning staff uniforms. Depending on the size of your facility, the staff can be enormous.

On the other hand, I've worked with tiny jurisdictions, too. One comes to mind where the Sheriff's wife does the cooking for the single digit numbers of incarcerated individuals they have in custody. Smaller correctional facilities can be just as complex as larger ones. In those settings, everyone wears multiple hats.

Large or small, it is imperative that you fully understand your facility. Here are a few questions to help you with this task:

What is the overall chain of command in the building?

What are the various departments?

What is the leadership structure in each department?

Where can you find the policies and procedures?

Who is responsible for making sure that educators know the policies and procedures?

These and other important questions must be answered. After orientation and once you get a handle on your teaching responsibilities, take time to build key relationships in your building. I tell new correctional educators that you will find allies, snitches, and reliable sources among your professional peers...use them all!

The power structure inside correctional facilities is different from more traditional jobs. Study it. Information is like currency, even among the incarcerated individuals. Become informed.

My friend Marie, a retired Deputy Chief in Maryland, enjoyed a 30 plus year career in corrections. She held multiple positions from a uniformed officer to retiring as a member of leadership. Her advice for correctional educators is to *"take advantage of any training that will strengthen your core competencies and advance your skills in multiple fields. Consider criminal justice, sociology or mental health; engage in cross-training opportunities to learn other areas of the operation."* Your employment situation will determine whether you can do this formally or informally, but I agree that expanding your skills and knowledge is an asset in our work.

I always built strong relationships. During lockdowns or other slow periods, I would talk to the folks in classification. This gave me a better understanding of my students. Housing placement could be adding unseen pressure or fears that might show up in my classroom. I needed to understand the complexities that they lived with. That is just one example.

THE MAIN POINT

As a correctional educator, your job is NOT the main function of the facility that you work in. Hands down the primary function of the correctional facility is CUSTODY AND SECURITY. You must get a grasp of how the system works. Your safety could depend on it.

MY "AHA" MOMENT

The education of my students was always extremely important to me early in my career. I ran into countless barriers and battles with other departments and specific staff who did not share my point of view. I was standing on my principles! These students deserved a second chance and at times it seemed that others in the building made my job harder.

I came to understand that in order to maintain my sanity (and keep my job), I must find a way to be a great teacher while playing nice with the various departments in the building. I began to slowly understand that each department and staff member had a job to do.

As I built strong relationships, I was able to reassure my peers that I was not some liberal, softy teacher who liked to "hug-a-thug." Have you heard of that one before? I proved that I was firm but fair with my students.

Once the uniformed staff recognized that Coach Smedley was not going to fall for inmate manipulation, we became a team. One time a particular student who smiled sweetly in my classroom, but regularly cursed at the Officer in the housing unit was surprised when Coach Smedley made a cameo appearance. I passed through the Sally port and stood beside the Officer as we had a quick "chat" about my student's behavior. The student needed to see that we (me and the Officer) were on the same page. I would use everything in my power to help this student get a job on the outside, but while he was inside he needed to learn respect.

I will admit that I had to get over myself as this Great Educator. I was essentially a guest in the Department of Correction's house. Fortunately, through careful "exploration" I found the path to sustaining life on Saturn and found that I loved it on this different planet.

Professional Development Activity

Have you ever taken a step back and examined your environment at work? Using *My Job Map* below we will practice our thinking muscles. The arrows flowing from you should represent the departments you interact with. The arrows flowing from the departments can be used to list any issues or challenges that you may be experiencing. Coach Smedley included an example for you. Remember, this is not personal. As professionals, we want to focus on the problem, not people. After you complete your map, next start thinking about <u>solutions.</u> Identifying a problem and then looking for solutions is a positive exercise. (Note – some problems are beyond your ability to solve them. In that case you have important employment decisions to make).

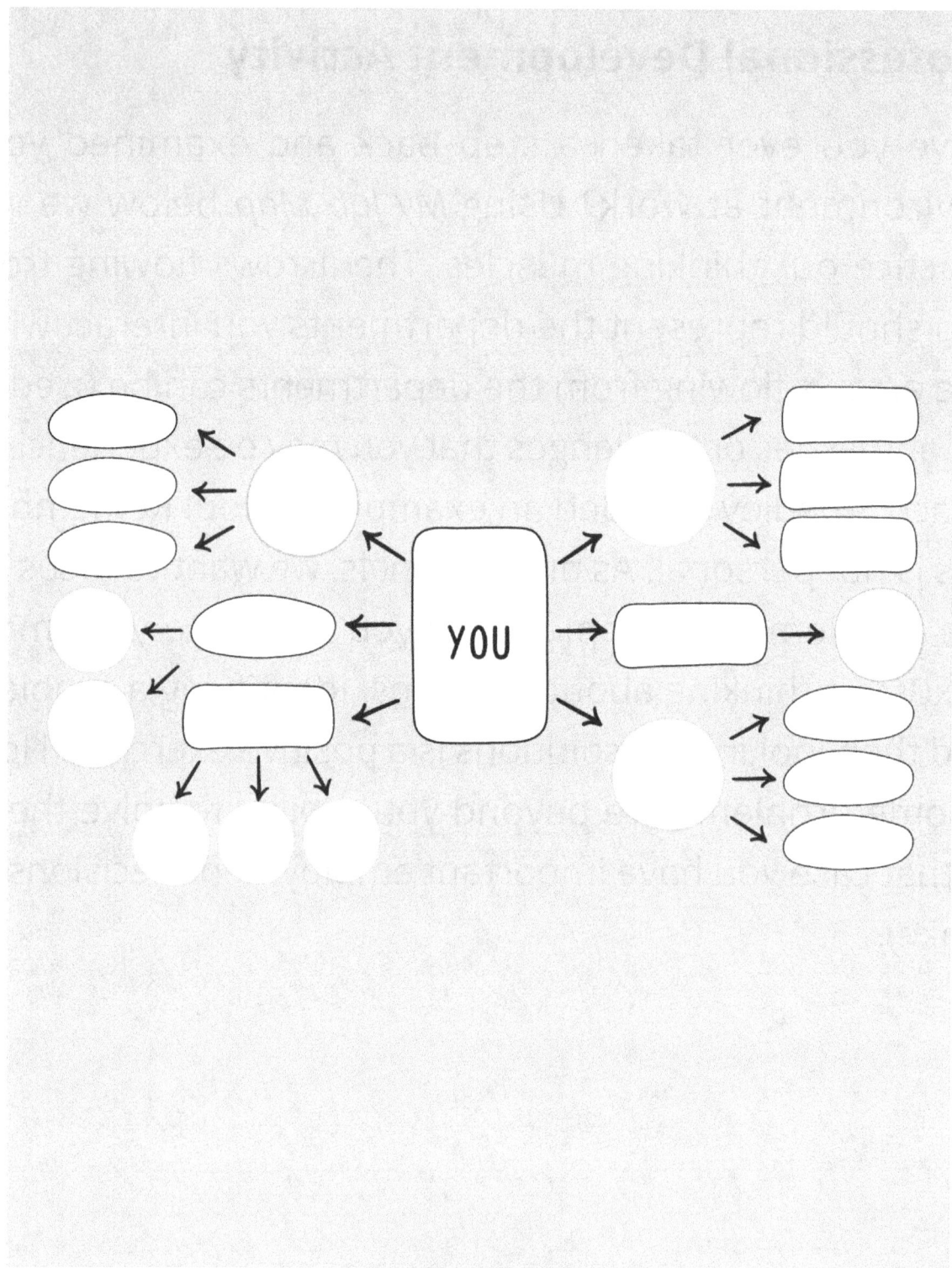

My Job Map

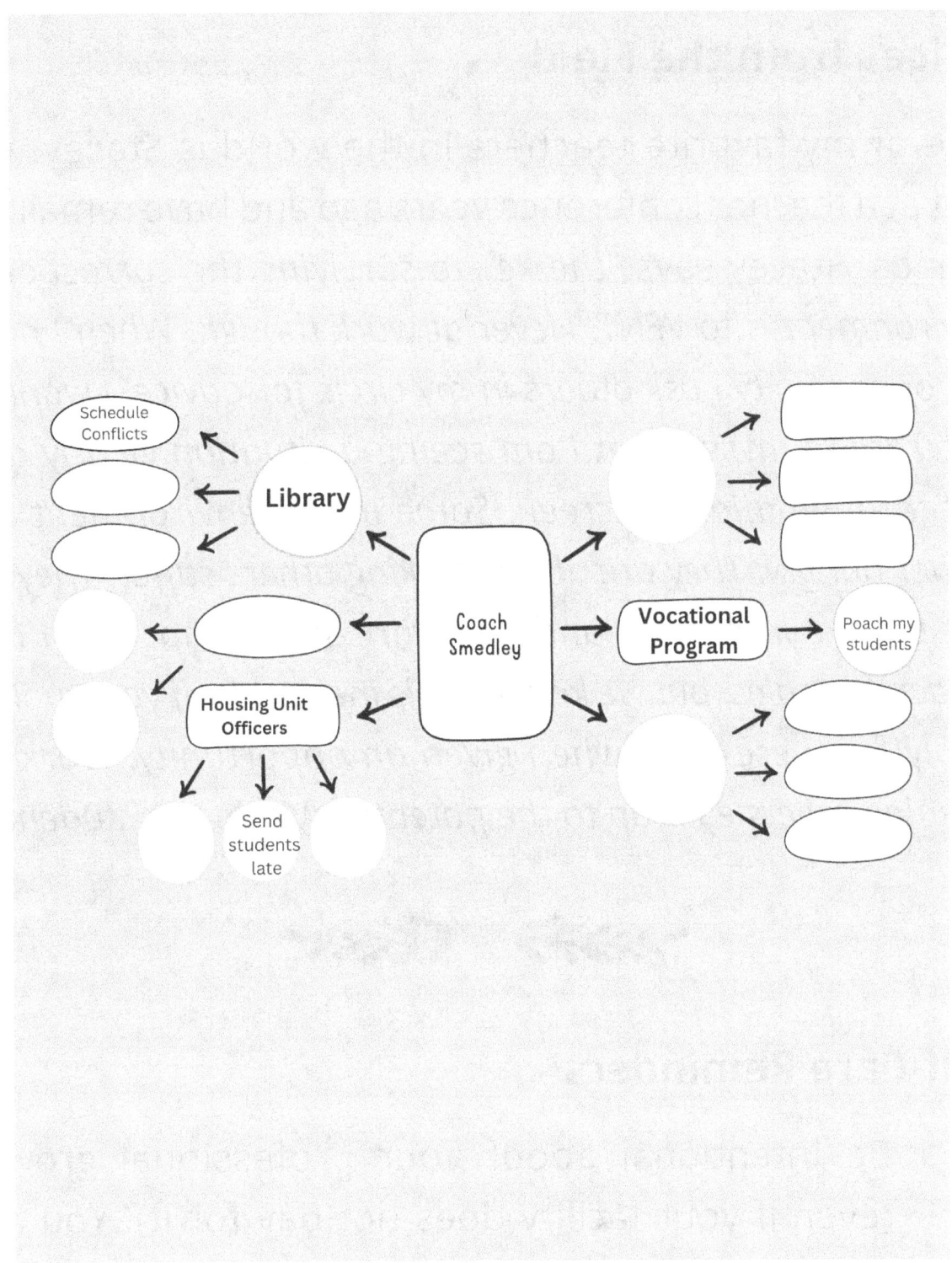

Coach Smedley's Job Map

Voices from the Field

One of my favorite teachers in the world is Stacey. We met at a teacher conference years ago and have remained friends. Stacey says "*the key to surviving the correctional environment is to VENT. Never at work though. When I have the opportunity I ask others in my circle for advice. I want to reiterate to myself that I am seeing a situation clearly and not through a jaded screen. Some in this environment are power hungry. They are about making others suffer. They do not believe in change and therefore should not be in any leadership roles, but we know this is inevitable. If you qualify, apply for these roles when given an opportunity. Work on opening others eyes up to the potential within our students.*"

Self-Care Reminders

1. Be intentional about your professional growth (even if your facility does not pay for it). You are worth the investment.

2. Reduce your stress. Journal, take long walks, med-

itate. You must find a place to release negativity. Your body, heart, or mind is not the place to store it.

3. Find your tribe. Actively build your support networks.

My Chapter 3 Reflection

4

One Room Schoolhouse

I can accept failure, everyone fails at something. But I can't accept not trying. Michael Jordan

W hen I hear the term "one room schoolhouse" I think of a scene from *"Little House on the Prairie."* The kind face of the teacher wearing those round spectacles comes to mind. That one room schoolhouse included big kids and little kids, all busily learning at their own level. That image feels very nostalgic. The reality of the one room schoolhouse in our world is not so romantic.

It can be overwhelming when you are in the classroom, especially in a carceral setting, with students who have vastly different abilities. In this situation you will encounter a range of students. From the student who wants to learn but needs tons of help, to the student who is very bright but doesn't think they need much help from you.

How do you manage your classroom, provide the structure that each student needs, while achieving all of your standards? And what about all of those different personalities?

If you are like I was, you are trying desperately to engage all of your students while they are bored, frustrated, or plotting some mischief. Just when you get a group of students on task, you look over and see that a student has fallen asleep in the back of the room. And then you notice that another group is playing spades! In that moment you are standing there, looking around your classroom and feeling like you are accomplishing absolutely nothing. We have all been there.

It starts with identifying the range of abilities among your students as early as you can. If you administer placement tests, you need to study how each student scored. Gathering intel at the beginning of your semester, cohort, or however your school year is divided up, will be a good investment of your time. If your class is not focused on equivalency, let's say, you teach life skills, find creative ways to figure out and measure what skill levels you are dealing with.

For example, I have new recruits complete a one paragraph writing assignment in the application packet. Usually, I will ask a general question like why they want to enroll in the program. Their response will quickly let me know their writing skills and give me a peek into their personal motivation. You can identify who will need more help, or who is highly advanced. With proper planning you can prepare for both types of students. You must gain this information as early as possible.

THE MAIN POINT

Having students of differing abilities in the same classroom can be a logistical challenge. The good news is that with some upfront preparation, careful planning, and knowing your students, you CAN build a strong learning community.

MY "AHA" MOMENT

After experiencing the one room school house phenomena, I developed a system. My system included three key elements:

1. Build a community in the classroom

2. Establish a culture of excellence

3. Teach to the middle, while providing support for the "edges"

Let's unpack each of these elements.

Build a Community in the Classroom

From the first day of class, I had students share generic information about themselves – favorite car, sports team, ice cream flavor, etc. as a way of relating to someone else in the room. Before they even know each other's names, they will have found some common interests. It is important to keep this early initiation light and fun. Being in the environment that we work in our students are hesitant and suspicious of others (including us) until they feel comfortable.

Once I established the ground rules and set the tone for my classroom, my job became much easier. It usually took about 2-3 weeks for students to build trust or lose interest and quit. I called that "thinning the crowd." It is the natural order of group dynamics in the incarcerated setting. In **Practical Topics in Correctional Education Vol. II** Coach Smedley will focus on more student engagement strategies, and hands-on activities. Here I want to focus on the big picture and how to establish your classroom management tactics from the beginning.

As students get to know one another in the early weeks, I often included questions about their career goals. It is great to see automotive guys finding one another, trades people talking about their construction skills, or tech nerds sharing industry information. You get the idea.

Each day I sprinkled in some aspect of learning and caring after one another. I reinforced that we were a team, a community. I established group rules about respect and helping each other early on. I also used games to build teamwork muscles and added a little friendly competition. Soon my AM class wondered how my PM class compared to them. Be careful with the competition, though. Some students are Type A personalities and are extremely competitive. You don't want to cause a security incident.

Establish a Culture of Excellence

This element will depend largely on how you carry yourself! Coach Smedley was established as a no nonsense, drill instructor-like teacher from my first encounter during recruitment. I give an overview of what to expect in class, what students will gain, and my methods used to build skills. I also make a point of telling new students that I am tough, but fair, and that I want them to win! At this point I reference some of my success stories with past students. On a few occasions I invited past students to call on the telephone and speak to current students (after clearing it with the Warden of course). These brief calls solidified my sincerity, effectiveness and genuine care for my students. If a call is not permissible, see if you can read written testimonials from past students who are now released or who have graduated from your program. Remember to remove any identifiers.

Armed with my clipboard, packets, and powerful message, I invite students to join me on a life changing journey. We speak at length about habits. I explicitly state that I will help them build habits for a successful life but remind them that I'm just their coach. When they get released, *they* become the quarterback of their own lives.

One thing about building a culture of excellence, you may first have to build your student's stamina. For example, a writing assignment for homework may start with three sentences, then a paragraph, then two paragraphs, ending up with one page of writing.

An important <u>secret</u> to engaging your correctional students is to EXPECT MORE FROM THEM THAN ANYONE ELSE EVER HAS! I had co-workers who were absolutely shocked that I could get students to complete: 1) homework; 2) projects; 3) weekend packets, etc. My students knew that I was invested in them. They did the work because I asked them to, and expected them to invest in themselves.

The road to success required them to build stamina and confidence. By connecting the dots between effort and accomplishment, I showed students that now was the time to educate themselves, while they had free time. They may never get this opportunity again! I reminded them that upon release, demands on their time would increase.

Coach Smedley's Classroom Rules

1. **Be On Time**

2. **Come Prepared**

3. **Be Willing to Try**

4. **Be Ready to Change**

Sample Classroom Rules

Teach to the Middle, Support the "Edges"

The last strategy that I used to survive the one room schoolhouse was teaching to the middle, while supporting the "edges." Let me explain. If I found that 80% of the students were learning and performing, I would then examine what was going on with the roughly 10% who did not understand and the other 10% who were more advanced.

For those two groups I would establish a plan. I might request volunteers to help those that needed it. If volunteers were not an option, I would schedule one-on-one time with the student(s) who needed extra help. For the students who were more advanced, I had two strategies. I would either give them a different independent assignment that was more challenging, or I would utilize them as a peer tutor if that did not violate any protocols or compromise security.

It is very wise to create and maintain materials for both groups of students who are on the "edges." You will frequently need to use those kinds of materials.

Once I got a firm idea of the skill levels of my students, I would begin to employ other strategies to promote growth. For example, if I identify that Jimmy is good at math, I might turn to Jimmy when the class is stumped with a math problem and say *"Jimmy, as our resident math whiz, please help your team out with the answer!"* Jimmy now takes pride in being acknowledged as competent in math. I also acknowledged characteristics beyond academics. *"Chris, thank you for helping the new student get caught up. I appreciate your leadership."*

I made a mental note to offer a positive observation or share a moment with each student at least once a week. It may be in the form of a public praise in front of the class, or a check-in to see how they are doing – *"how's your mom feeling, Caitlyn? I remember last class you were worried about her."* Simply remembering and acknowledging something important to your student goes a very long way.

One cautionary note on public praise. I purposely spread those around evenly among several students. If you are always praising the same student, in the carceral setting you may unwittingly put a target on their back. Our students can be jealous, sneaky, and prone to bullying others. Look for warning signs of those traits in your classroom community.

You can neutralize behavior like that by gently addressing it using motivational interviewing techniques. We can remind students that being part of our learning community is causing them to change. Our collaborative goal is for them to go home as a different person than the one who entered the correctional facility. In the article "Understanding Motivational Interviewing" Dr. Elizabeth Hartney reminds us of an important principle of motivational interviewing. *"Developing discrepancy is based on the belief that a person becomes more motivated to change once they see the mismatch between where they are and where they want to be. It is a counselor's job to help clients and clarify their personal goals. Goals and actions are developed in a trusting, collaborative atmosphere free from pressure. This offers an environment that is based on the person's needs, wishes, goals, values, and strengths."*

Teaching in a one room schoolhouse can be a challenge. The correctional educator who remains committed to reaching all students, and gets themselves organized can triumph over the challenge.

Professional Development Activity

The best advice I can give you regarding the one room schoolhouse is to get organized. The second piece of advice is to learn how to include all skill levels in the classroom. One idea that has worked for me is the **group project**. I take a big topic we are covering in class and divide it into smaller activities. I then allow students to select how they want to participate. One group watches video(s), another does research, a third group may write a script for role play. The sky is the limit. You may need to create packets, but make them reusable. Here is an example of a project Coach Smedley used. Using the blank form, think of a supplemental activity that you can easily add to your classroom. (Note: don't feel as if you need a special project every week. Create and use them as you have time and energy).

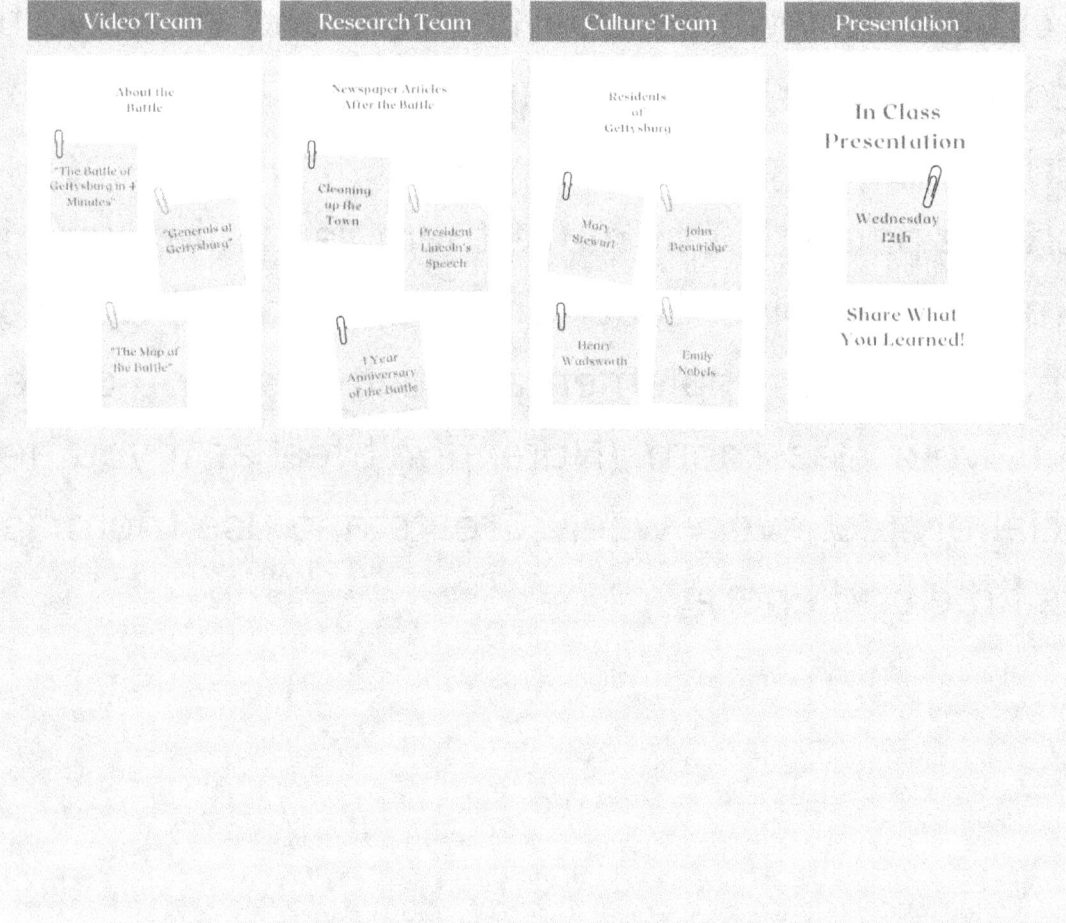

Sample Group Project Plan

Project:_____

			Presentation Info
Topic 1	Topic 2	Topic 3	
			Share What You Learned!

Blank Group Project Plan

Voices from the Field

"The best correctional educators are patient, have a sense of humor, and are full of compassion and enthusiasm," Angel from New Jersey says. Angel is another friend that I connected with at a teacher conference at least ten years ago. Regarding the huge range of different skill levels in class, Angel says *"I incorporate creative activities appropriate for all academic levels. Creativity relieves stress, improves cognitive function, and nurtures confidence in our students."*

Self-Care Reminders

1. Get organized to help you avoid feeling overwhelmed.

2. Ask for help. If volunteers are available at your facility, make use of them to help students who need more support.

3. Celebrate your victories! Remember that a small win is still a win.

My Chapter 4 Reflection

5

Your Amazing Space

That is what learning is. You suddenly understand something you've understood all your life, but in a new way. Doris Lessing

Imagine you are a sixth grader. It is a typical evening at your house – with your grown-ups drinking, arguing, and hitting. The chaos and noise last late into the night and you can finally go to bed after the police leave. After only a few hours of sleep you get dressed and go to school. Or you don't go to school and sleep all day due to exhaustion and stress. Many of our students have lived this scenario or something similar throughout their childhood.

One of the reasons that students drift away from an interest in school is the fact that they could not consistently get a good night's sleep and a warm breakfast to prepare them for learning at school. Whether this lack of preparation is caused by violence, neglect, or both, these students find themselves uncomfortable in the classroom. Another version of this story is the kid who is still in pain from the bruises or injuries they may have sustained.

Many of the adult learners that we see today carry baggage from these past experiences. During orientation I always ask prospective students when they stopped liking school. The answer that I usually get is 4th grade. This puzzled me for years until I started connecting the dots. If home is not safe, and I don't feel like I fit in at school, it is very easy to fall into the "lure" of the streets. Crime and gangs welcome everybody! No experience needed.

Once I understood these obstacles that our students face, I developed an effective strategy of energizing my classroom space. I set out to recreate the elements of creativity and curiosity that made them feel good when they entered the classroom as children. Bright colors, interesting learning centers, informative posters, etc. all contributed to creating this safe and fun space. Several students indicated that when they came to class "it didn't feel like I was in jail anymore."

Our spaces should be clean and organized. Even in older buildings we can create a positive atmosphere. This is not about having the most high-tech furniture or equipment.

You can literally transform any space into a learning environment if you really try. And before you begin to worry that finding time to build an amazing space is too difficult, let me assure you that with a little planning, set up, and maintenance you can build and sustain the space that I am describing.

The activities in this chapter will help you with planning and maintaining your energized space. Practical ideas include changing your learning stations either every few months or before each new cohort, the choice is up to you. You can also simply refresh your centers by restocking handouts, or change the images on displays, or update positive affirmations regularly. More on this topic later.

First things first. **What you teach does not keep you from using some of these ideas**. You may have to tweak an idea based on your subject matter or security protocols, but know that you can creatively make any subject interesting. Also, keep in mind that many of the **adulting skills** that we learned came from our homes, our high schools, or our first jobs. These institutions provided a foundation of knowledge that we utilize in our daily lives – personally and professionally. If a student experienced disruption within any of these systems, they will have "gaps" of information. By implementing warm up activities, independent projects, or simulations we can fill in some of those gaps. The great news is that we can do so without taking away time from our required curriculum. Our incarcerated learners have the benefit of TIME. Help them put this resource to good use!

After orientation I would slowly build my student's stamina. Many of them needed to shake off the rust because they had been out of school for a long time. Just like getting them into physical shape, I told my students that together we would get them into academic shape. I used many tools to get them in shape. I started with short warm up activities, moved into short homework assignments and eventually grew into longer projects using weekend packets.

THE MAIN POINT

We are in a unique position to influence our student's academic journey. Prior to incarceration, many of them did not have the environment to study, learn, and achieve. The causes may have been due to the

chaos in their lives, a parent's own illiteracy, or even an unstable housing situation. Correctional educators can stabilize our students by building skills and providing a nurturing environment. We can teach and develop good habits while stimulating their lifelong learning muscles!

MY "AHA" MOMENT

I discovered how important it is to fully understanding my student's past experiences with education. I could carefully incorporate into our daily routine the habits, behaviors, and knowledge that would get them closer to success. Most of the hard work is done once you establish your space and activate their natural curiosity.

Once you have the space, you can subtly begin to teach your students good habits around keeping the space neat and organized. We did a five-minute clean up before the end of class. I stressed that this will be a good habit when they get a job, to check your area, put your materials away and clean your workstation. This was done every time they exited our classroom. Over time I did not have to say anything, the students began to automatically start putting the classroom in order themselves. As teachers we just need to establish the expectation, demonstrate how it is done, and remind the students to complete the task until it becomes second nature. The leaders will emerge and the group will start managing itself. Just watch.

Here are some practical ideas for creating your amazing space:

- Images – include positive affirmations, quotes, funny memes, etc. These can be used as discussion topics, artistic assignments by asking students to create original work, or material for writing an essay

- Industry Highlights – graphic of career pathways for attainable jobs, short articles about people or businesses

- Resource Boards – listing local places to turn to for help, handout outlining how to make a call and gather information (our students need this skill!)

- Skills Spotlight – have a learning center about skills

that employers want. Students can self-evaluate using a questionnaire, and simulate the skill with an independent activity. One example is to have them pretend to be a hiring manager and review a mock job description and/or review a sample candidate resume and make a hiring decision. This will prepare them for their own job search by helping them to think like an employer.

- Life Skills Display – our students need more practical life skills information. This area can focus on basic skills. Examples include – how to purchase a refrigerator, how to use a washing machine (fabric settings, detergents, etc.), how to clean a house or apartment (room by room checklist)

- Healthcare – a learning center on basic hygiene, preventive care, annual check-ups, etc. You can download or request free information from national organizations to stock this center

- Personal Finances – keep articles, handouts, or videos on budgeting, credit, the cost of using payday loans, etc.

- Family and Relationship – provide information on dating tips, parenting, marriage, etc

- Organizational Tools – this can be a learning center, or including good habits woven into the classroom schedule. Maintaining a calendar, planning a family outing, or planning a group project are good examples

Professional Development Activity

The best advice I can give you regarding the one room schoolhouse is to get organized. The second piece of advice is to learn how to include all skill levels in the classroom. One idea that has worked for me is the **group project**. I take a big topic we are covering in class and divide it into smaller projects and alloww students to pick their project. The whole thing comes together as a classroom presentation. Students learn to plan, research, write, and public speaking all in one activity. Having a choice of how to participate is empowering for students and helps to build their confidence. Study my classroom design and think of ways you can build energetic engagement in your space, too. Take a blank sheet of paper and work on your floorplan.

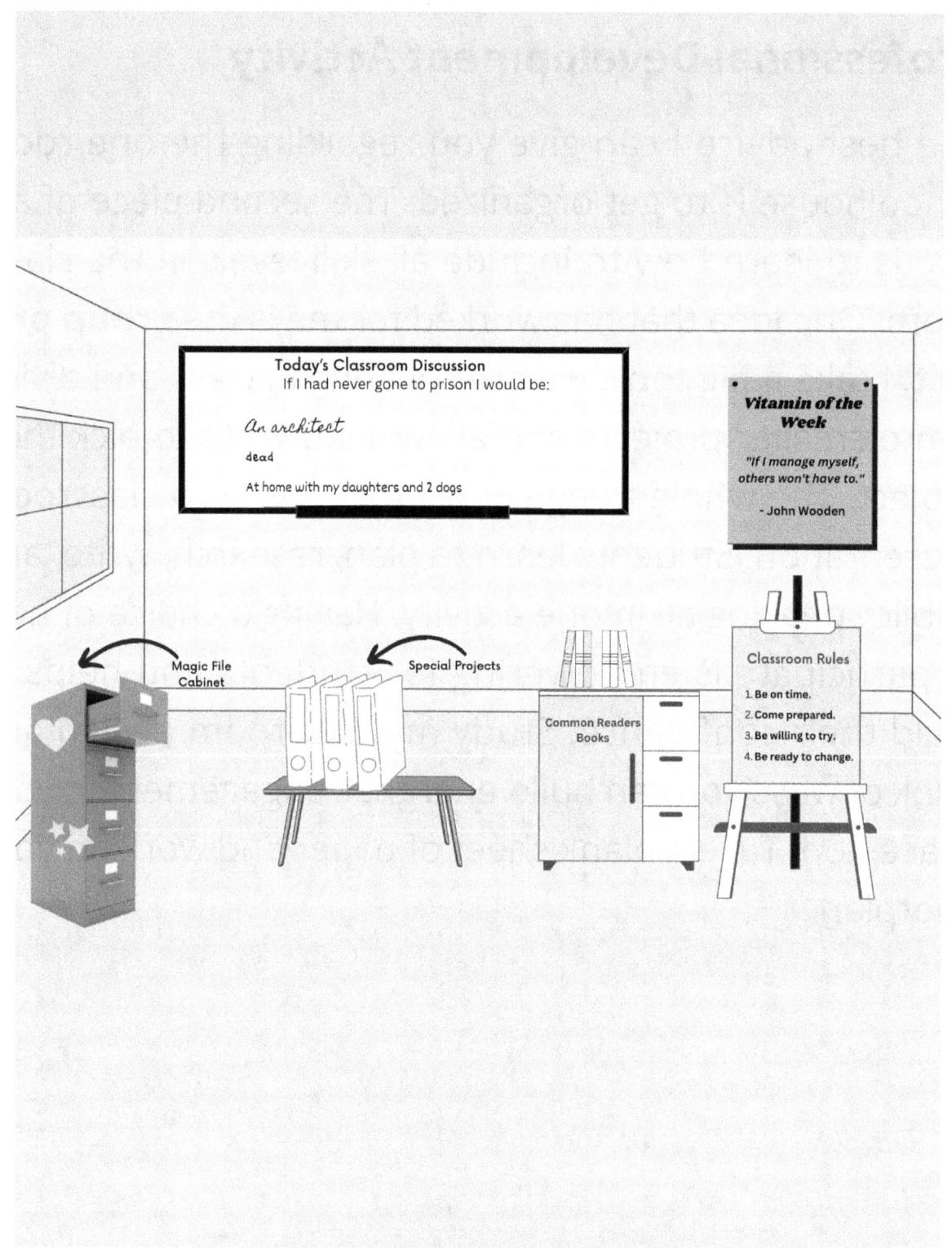

Coach Smedley's Classroom

Voices from the Field

One of my strongest tools for student engagement is an inviting space. For this topic, I will include my own voice. *"I always put care into designing my classroom. I even had maintenance hang images on the ceiling because I noticed some students looking up blankly when I was boring them. Once we put Van Gogh's Starry Night up there. A student wondered what it was. That question opened a whole new world of classic painters up to him. It worked. I was simply engaging students in a different way. "*

Self-Care Reminders

1. Keep a peaceful, clean, and pleasant classroom to help you stay centered.

2. Start an image file of motivational, inspirational, and/or beautiful images. They can be used with your class or keep them to yourself as you refresh during breaks. Either digital or print files work.

3. Listen to interesting podcasts.

My Chapter 5 Reflection

6

Recruiting for Your Program

The only recognizable feature of hope is action. Grace Paley

Think about the last time you interacted with a salesperson. The key question is did they annoy you or did they help you? Working with a salesperson who actually helps you can be the best experience ever! Being the helpful salesperson is an important, but not often discussed, aspect of your job. You need to master sales skills as you recruit for your program. HINT: the argument *"But it will be good for you"* is NOT enough to attract most student candidates.

I regret to inform you that you absolutely must know how to sell your program to potential students! Making a sale or getting to a "Yes" as you offer a product or service is fundamental to successful programs. Fortunately, it is a skill that can be developed. In Chapter 2 you learned that Coach Smedley was once a real estate agent in a past career. Without knowing it, my sales instincts helped me when I began my career in correctional education.

Flashback to one of my early recruiting experiences. I had been on the job for three weeks. I was told to set up in the day room where candidates from various housing units would be sent to me. I stood there waiting to make a presentation about our terrific program. I had the PowerPoint ready to go, handouts copied, and empty chairs waiting for occupants.

Over the next hour half sleepy, grumpy men filed into the room. They were told to report to a required meeting. Most were irritated and confused. *"What is this about*?" they asked. As a trained speaker, I knew how to engage them. Unfortunately, just as I got the group interested, another group arrived. Over and over, different housing units reported to the day room, each time disrupting the flow that I had started. It was a mess. And it was the last time I recruited that way.

I immediately asked the Warden to indulge me and allow me to try something different. I assured the Warden that I knew how to get our numbers, but it would require a different approach. Once given the greenlight, here is what Coach Smedley did:

1. Coordinated a visit to each housing unit

2. Developed a process that I repeated in each housing unit

3. Dedicated two days for recruitment

Rather than having candidates travel across the facility to hear some unknown presentation by an unknown lady, Coach Smedley went mobile. I wore my comfortable shoes, grabbed a clipboard and paperwork and hit the pavement. Once the candidates were assembled, I gave a brief presentation, asked for sign-ups and dismissed those who were not interested. They could get back to their sleep. The whole process took about 15-20 minutes. The process was done quarterly and became more efficient with each round.

The solution was actually pretty simple. I streamlined the process, removed the disruption of inmate movement, and delivered the message in a professional manner. Easy peazy.

Let's deep dive into the presentation itself. First, I informed the candidates *why* they were on my list *("You meet the criteria for eligibility for the program.").* Next, I reviewed *what* the program was, benefits to them, our expectations, and next steps. In other words, I painted a picture. Then I asked for the sale *("If you want to pursue this opportunity, we would love to have you, class starts next week. Would you like to sign up?").*

What happened next is critical to mention. Some candidates immediately signed up; others began giving excuses as to why they did not want to sign up. I simply asked for their initials in the Yes or No column. No convincing, no nagging. A moment of truth was all I was looking for. I quickly dismissed those that declined. Those who remained in the room were given a few more details and handed the application packet. I promised to return at a set day and time to collect the application. And then Coach Smedley would leave.

My follow-up visit took even less time. I would return to the housing unit when I said I would. That is important – do what you say you will do. You will quickly build credibility.

Candidates who handed me completed applications were given a welcome letter. The welcome letter contained the day/time to report to class and instructions to bring the letter with them on the first day. And then Coach Smedley would welcome them to the learning community. Candidates who did NOT complete the application were told that they *might* be seen in the next recruitment cycle and then Coach Smedley would leave.

The ingredients for this successful formula were simple. Accountability, professionalism, and kindness. I conducted the recruitment with precision and focus. It also helped when I acknowledged current students while I was in the housing units and spent a few minutes of friendly conversation with them. Candidates were watching; and noticing the rapport I had with my students. You are always being watched in a correctional facility, so use this knowledge to your advantage.

The last step in the recruitment process was the First Day. I greeted each new recruit at the door and collected their welcome letter. This simple form letter was a symbol of <u>acceptance</u> for the new students. Think about it, most of our students never get *positive written correspondence*.

They are used to getting a summons, warrant, ticket, court order, etc. My simple welcome letter was the equivalent of a college acceptance letter for many of them! Small gestures like that can set the tone for the student experience in your classroom.

The other strategy at work with the welcome letter is for new students to begin following your instructions. When possible, I would send students back to their housing unit if they forgot the letter. Or I would threaten that they might be removed from class if they did not bring the letter on the next day of class (totally a bluff, but it worked). The point is to start off from the very beginning creating compliance to your rules.

THE MAIN POINT

After a disastrous recruiting campaign, I learned how to deliver good customer service, paint a picture of the opportunity being offered, and close the deal with motivated students. By recruiting this way, new students could feel that this program was somehow different because I was not trying to convince them to sign up.

MY "AHA" MOMENT

I realized during this experience that people want to be involved in something structured and successful. You must earn their trust and learn what motivates them as quickly as possible. That will set the stage for each new cohort. By separating the recruitment process into three distinct touchpoints, the candidates weeded themselves out. Let's review the three touchpoints:

The Opportunity – I informed the candidates why they were selected. I covered the curriculum, expectations regarding attendance and participation, and past success stories. Again, I painted a picture and helped them to imagine themselves inside of it.

The Test – returning to pick up the application was a test. Candidates could have completed it during my first visit, but I did not do that. Some people will go through the motions with no intention of showing up on the first day of class. It is easy to check a box and sign up, but doing the application is work. <u>Put them to work and see what happens!</u> Slackers are shocked when I say that they *may* been seen next time. It is better to identify them early on before they drop out and effect your program numbers.

The First Day – by the first day of class candidates will have seen Coach Smedley three times. I have been consistent, pleasant, and inviting during each encounter. They are slowly learning that I can be trusted. If your schedule does not permit multiple visits over days, then at the very least return that afternoon. Separating the touchpoints is effective even with a shortened timeframe.

Another general observation of the recruitment process includes being student-centered. Help them to *feel* the benefits of joining your program. One example is from a time when I was the Life Skills Coordinator at a juvenile facility in the community. I wanted the students to learn about buying a car, so I took them on a field trip. We went to a new car lot where students were given a tour and had their pictures taken behind the wheel of a new car. We then went to a used car lot and got training on how to inspect a used car before making a purchase. The first stop was to help my students to dream, while the second stop was to provide them with practical information.

Incorporating the combination of emotional and practical information will have a big impact on your program. Retention will occur organically if you remember to reach your students on many levels.

In this section I have outlined strategies that worked well for me. You may have discovered totally different approaches that work in your region or your facility. Find methods that work best for you. The key takeaway is to understand that weeding out those who are not serious should be done early in the process. Having a few soft expectations built into your recruitment will help with the weeding out process.

Professional Development Activity

As a correctional educator you are selling your students a dream. Whether that dream is a high school equivalency, college credit, a vocational certification, etc. it is a distant, hard to imagine idea. The blank idea form below can help you to think about ways to sell your program to potential students. Think about selling points. Why should a potential student think about signing up for the program? What will convince them?

Recruiting Ideas

Benefits of Program

Blank Idea form

Voices from the Field

I have a friend named Bob who was a vocational teacher in Virginia. For years Bob worked with the female population. He prepared them for non-traditional work in the construction trades. Bob told me "*my first task was to help the students remember how to dream. They had to picture themselves doing this work. I encouraged them to learn their trade well, because they would work around guys who wouldn't always respect them. After years of losing – many had been trafficked, abused, just thrown away – so now my job was to teach them to be winners. Maybe for the first time in their lives! I did have to eliminate the slackers, but after that, the students worked hard to build new lives in a high paying job.*"

Self-Care Reminders

1. Recognize busy seasons at your job. Be sure to go the extra mile to stay hydrated, nourished, and calm. Reward yourself with something special after

you get through the busy season.

2. During periods of high student contact, it is impera- tive to keep your batteries charged. Many students that you encounter will be negative, broken, and perhaps hostile. This can be draining! You must have your highest and best energy available during this time. Also have a plan to recover *after* days like this. I would look forward to going swimming after recruitment was over.

3. Take inventory of your mental health. Working in corrections is not conducive to having bad days that make you vulnerable. When you are not focused, or going through something, you may share too much, or let your guard down. Some incarcerated individ- uals will move in and pounce when they sense your vulnerability. When possible, remove yourself from the environment when you are off balance.

My Chapter 6 Reflection

7

"Dear Coach, I Need Toilet Paper!"

The sidelines are not where you want to live your life. The world needs you in the arena. Tim Cook

The message sounded urgent. A young man, who I did not know, sent me a frantic message through the fancy new tablets my facility was testing. He had sent the same message to me three times, within minutes of each other. His message raised so many questions. Who was this person? Was I the only recipient of his message? Did solving this most basic human need now rest on my shoulders?

His message caught me off guard because I was not an official staff member, I was only a contractor. Apparently, every professional staff member in the building was listed as a contact on this tablet. In addition, my role was to teach job search skills. I ran groups on preparing resumes, interview tips, and how to think like an employer. (*"If you were an employer, would you hire you?"* I would often ask my students). The point is that I had nothing to do with internal jail stuff. And yet, somehow this young stranger imagined that I could solve his important problem.

I responded quickly to the young man who needed toilet paper. I explained to him that I was not the person to contact but offered to send a message to the appropriate staff person. And then I followed up by actually sending the message, right then and there. I never learned what happened next, but I sure hope that he got that toilet paper.

This scenario was not the last time that I would be approached to help fix a situation where I had no authority. In almost every facility where I have ever worked, Coach Smedley got a reputation for being a problem-solver. Generally, I think that's a good thing, but I have had to learn discretion.

Coach Smedley has been told many times to *'stay in your lane'* or *'you're doing too much.'* I also heard a few *'they don't pay me enough to work that hard.'* One staff person actually pulled me aside and told me that I shouldn't waste my time with these students. I am always more than a little suspicious when people go out of their way to offer me unsolicited career advice.

On this subject I will say one thing – you must determine for yourself the type of teacher you want to be. If it is just a job you behave one way; but if you are like Coach Smedley and it is a calling...that is a different matter.

THE MAIN POINT

You can make enemies in the correctional setting if you are not careful. You cannot be seen as too inmate-friendly because it can weaken your effectiveness. The best thing you can do is to build strong relationships with your healthy co-workers, always carry yourself as a professional, and be consistent. Over time your reputation will grow among staff and incarcerated individuals alike.

MY "AHA" MOMENT

In one facility where I worked my program was very successful. I had a waiting list of candidates waiting to get in. Initially my haters (I've had them at literally every job I have ever had) accused me of misdeeds. The wild accusations varied from I must be letting them use the telephones, or I must be sneaking in contraband, or I must be sleeping with some of them. That was the only way some co-workers could comprehend my success. None of those accusations were true, by the way. My success happened because I genuinely cared about my students, I was well read and informed about best practices. It also helped that I had personal family experience with incarceration. My father started a fifteen year prison sentence when I was ten-years-old.

I was offended by the rumors but did not allow them to hinder my work. You must remember this fact - excellence and competence will always attract critics.

This chapter deals with when and how to **advocate** for your students. An early lesson that you will learn is that you must avoid inmate manipulation. Coach Smedley totally agrees with this premise. However, everything is NOT inmate manipulation. A student who needs toilet paper is a basic human need. Period.

Our students may often be impatient and sometimes annoying with their approach, but I always try to weigh the situation at hand. My personal philosophy is that kindness is NOT falling for inmate trickery. You will walk a tightrope when it comes to this issue. My advice would be to stay true to your philosophy and keep your integrity. Know the boundaries and never blur the lines.

Knowing when to advocate and when to stand down is a skill you will hopefully learn within your first few years. Every battle that you witness is not worth "dying" for. An important lesson learned in this area is knowing which student(s) to go to bat for. If you insert yourself into jail or prison business to support a student, you had better be backing a winning horse. You will find egg on your face if that particular student ever does anything after you have advocated for them. Believe me, I know. Years later that student's name will be thrown in your face as evidence that you were fooled. Never mind that ninety-nine of your other students have changed, and gone on to stay out of trouble, that one student will haunt you. Your co-workers will make sure of it.

Save your intervention for truly critical instances. My Warden got to know me very well over the course of working together for several years. She knew that if I raised an issue, it must be important. I gained her trust because:

- I did not over-react

- If I made a mistake I owned up to it immediately – you read about one instance in Chapter 1.

- I never forgot the prime directive - custody and security

As deeply as I cared for my students, I always tried to size up situations through the lens of custody and security. I truly hope that most of you will not find yourselves the target of such cruelty and pettiness. If you do, I highly recommend that you maintain a strong network away from the job. Coach Smedley is fortunate to have both a close-knit family AND a broad network of loyal peers. I was born into the family, but I developed the peer network with intentionality. And you can, too.

Professional Development Activity

In correctional education we walk a fine line between being too soft on criminals, or being a part of a criminal legal system that is not working. You must find your lane and define for yourself what is important to you. In this activity list the core principles that you believe in. Knowing your beliefs about the work will guide you as situations arise. Think about your views on corrections, humane treatment, second chances, etc.

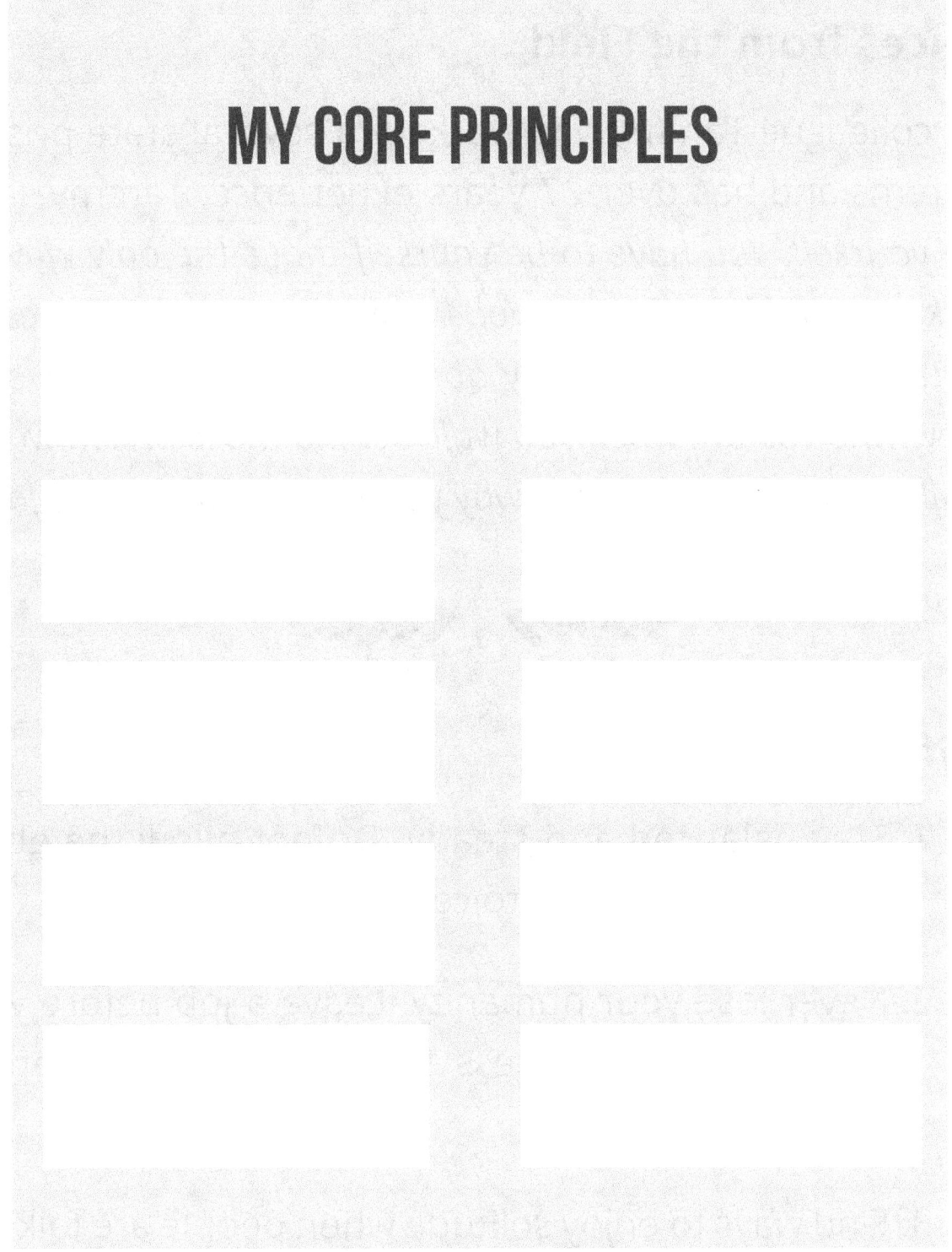

My Core Principles

Voices from the Field

My colleague Tammy has worked in several state prison systems and has over 27 years experience. Tammy says *"Be yourself. You have to be yourself that's the only way to make it behind the wall. Do you know who you are? It doesn't matter what co-workers say about you. You really have to know who you are when you walk behind those prison walls. It will keep you grounded in why you are here at this the job."*

Self-Care Reminders

1. Stay balanced and steady. Do not allow the ebbs and flows of the job to cause you to move.

2. Never lose your humanity. Leave a job before you lose your soul! Kindness and compassion are forms of strength, too.

3. Find ways to enjoy solitude when people are talking about you. Cultivate your inner strength.

My Chapter 7 Reflection

8

Special Interests

The whole secret of life is to be interested in one thing profoundly and in a thousand things well. Horace Walpole

As the parent of a child on the spectrum, I found myself having to learn a whole new language. One term that always interested me was "special interest." Children and young adults on the spectrum often develop special interests around random topics. As they pursue a new special interest, they go big! For example, one year my daughter was really into stamp collecting. We bought a fancy stamp collector kit which included a stamp album, tweezers, and a magnifying glass. We visited the national postal museum (a real place in Washington, DC!). She wanted all things related to postal stamps...until she moved on to her next special interest. These projects with my kid gave us special time together AND developed her academic curiosity. Today she is a college student who owns a catalog of experiential knowledge that few students her age possess.

My takeaway from that experience is that pursuing a special interest could be a great exercise for our students in correctional education. I began to utilize the concept of special interest in my classroom. Since they were adult learners, projects would be more independent, but I imagined that they would have the same positive results. Over time, I discovered another important benefit of encouraging my students to pursue special interests – my own self-care! Let me explain.

Bringing YOUR Special Interests into the Classroom

What are you passionate about? When you love something – sports, gardening, pottery, or whatever, your energy is contagious. Bring your passion to the job. Why? Well, because the things that you are interested in will also grab your student's attention. The other thing about bringing your passion into the classroom is that it makes you happy. When you have a bad day and you can spend time talking about a topic that interests you, it is a form of self-care for you in that moment. You are basically bringing some happiness and joy into the classroom space.

I know we are always told not to share personal information. I am not suggesting that you do that. Talking about gardening is not revealing any of your personal information. Now if you say that you go to the Home Depot on Elm Street every Saturday to buy gardening supplies, well, don't do that! That is an example of over-sharing. General conversation about basic gardening would be acceptable.

My thing is history. I would like to think that over the years I have encouraged some history buffs out there. Whether it's talking about Gettysburg or the American Revolution or the invention of the printing press, Coach Smedley always manages to sprinkle in a little history into our lesson. I bring history alive through storytelling, by comparing history to present day events, and along the way students also get valuable opportunities for reading.

Why Special Interest Projects Work

Many correctional students have "gaps" in their education. Special interests provide the opportunity to fill these gaps with cool new information. Think about it. Many of our students have never been exposed to the broader world – in terms of geography, culture, languages, and many others wonderful ways to explore our planet.

Exploring a variety of topics will also give our students something to talk about as they reenter society. One thing that I have always heard my students talk about is getting a "real job" and how uncomfortable they feel around "regular" people. They are trying to articulate the fact that outside of criminal and street activity, many times they feel like a fish out of water. I gently share with my students that real life is pretty plain, sometimes even boring. What they perceive as the "excitement" of criminal activity can be replaced with many safer and simpler options that won't land them behind bars.

I once asked a group of students what they did in their spare time, as a hobby. One student raised his hand and said *"That's easy, Coach Smedley. I smoke weed!"* I proceeded to inform my student that depending on what state he lived in, that might be a new charge! So, I asked the better question - "*What is a hobby?*"

This dialogue opened the door to all kinds of interesting possibilities with my students. I created a workshop *Finding Your Hobby*. My students learned that not only does a hobby contribute to good health by providing stress relief, but it can also tap into hidden talents and create income earning opportunities. Hobbies can also develop patience and build character.

We discussed all types of potential hobbies and special interests. Birdwatching, kayaking, photography, square dancing, etc. The list of possibilities was endless. In my *Finding Your Hobby* workshop I organized hobbies by cost, showing free or low cost to more expensive options. This helped my students to think about what it would take to pursue a new hobby or special interest.

THE MAIN POINT

General knowledge is a wonderful gift that you can give to your students! They can have something to talk about at lunchtime on their job, whether it's a warehouse or an office or a fast-food restaurant. It feels good to know stuff! To have something to contribute to the conversation. If our students learn basic information that "regular" people know, that will help them to reintegrate back into society more naturally. The benefit for you is that you get to share something that brings you joy with your students in a meaningful way.

MY "AHA" MOMENT

After being treated to see *"Hamilton"* for my birthday, I returned to work and found clips from the musical on YouTube. I played these clips for my students and watched their fascination. Many knew some of the hip hop songs that were covered in the show. Others loved the fast-paced rapping. A few even enjoyed the retelling of the story of the American Revolution. They wanted to know how they could attend a musical, as many had never done so. Once again, a few minutes during class gave the students a glimpse into a whole new world.

Another example comes from my fifth-grade teacher. I remember her playing the guitar in class in the afternoons. She would tie the songs she played to our lesson. I can still sing *Aloha Oe* from our geography lesson about Hawaii. Most importantly she fascinated us with stories of playing in a folk band while she was in college. I never forgot the emotional connection she made with us. She got my young mind thinking about college life with her vivid stories. We can have the same effect on our adult learners by sharing our passion with them.

Ways that Students Benefit from Special Interests

- Reinforce basic skills

- Awareness of current events

- Increase cultural competence

- Develop independent work habits

- Identify hidden skills, interests and abilities

- Promote lifelong learning

After you get students thinking about finding their own special interests or hobbies, you can get creative about how to incorporate them into your curriculum. Here are a few examples:

- Charts and Statistics. While discussing the pandemic, I had students review statistics about how many people died during the pandemic in the 19th century. This was helpful to prepare them for equivalency exams where they would have to interpret charts.

- Student in-class "mail." I had a student who loved cars and engines, a real gear head. I saw a magazine article about a new type of engine. I printed the one-page article, and I gave it to him. It was his in-class mail for the week. Every student received a unique piece of mail based on their interests. Zero class time is used for this activity, and you determine the frequency of how often you deliver the mail (weekly, bi-weekly, or even monthly). This will further connect students to your class. Topics can be fun, informative, or more serious. I once gave a handout about the long-term effects of smoking marijuana to a youth student.

- Weekend/Homework packets. Assign or have students select a topic to research over the weekend or as homework projects. The packet should have general information and something for students to complete when they return the packet - worksheets, essay questions, quizzes, etc. Keep a blank master packet for future use. You will just need to replenish the consumable handouts.

Best Practices/Points to Remember

You can add special interest activities without a great deal of extra work for yourself. My **Magic File Cabinet** approach is to create a lesson once, and carefully preserve all of the materials for future classes of students. I can go to my magic file cabinet and produce an activity on demand. Over the years my magic file cabinet has become an invaluable resource.

As you discuss your passion special interest, remember to start at the beginning. I had a teacher tell me he tried to introduce golfing to a class and the activity bombed. After a few questions I identified what went wrong. The teacher had begun talking about The Masters events, and the history of golf. Boring!! I theorized that his students did not know anything about golf and felt insecure. (And the information was boring!).

You never want students to feel like they are the only ones in the room who doesn't know something. Most of the students were aware of golf, having heard that business deals are made on the golf course through pop culture. What they didn't know was anything about the basics of the game. I suggested that the teacher explain how golf balls are made, the speed of the golf ball, how the golf course is laid out (students with landscaping backgrounds will perk up and listen). You must connect the information to something from their world. Next, you must explain the basics or important background information. If you make it relevant, interesting, and fun your students will take it from there.

Final thought – if your facility has a library, coordinate with the librarian to have a special display featuring materials about the special interest topic. After you plant the seed, students will inevitably want to pursue more information on their own.

Professional Development Activity

Sharing your hobby or special interest with your students can richly add to their knowledge and skills. You can do something as simple as share a magazine article, do a mini workshop, or assign a group activity around a current event. Get creative! List your special interests on the blank form. I completed the form with actual special interests that have been used in my classroom over the years. After identifying an interest, think of a way to introduce it into your teaching.

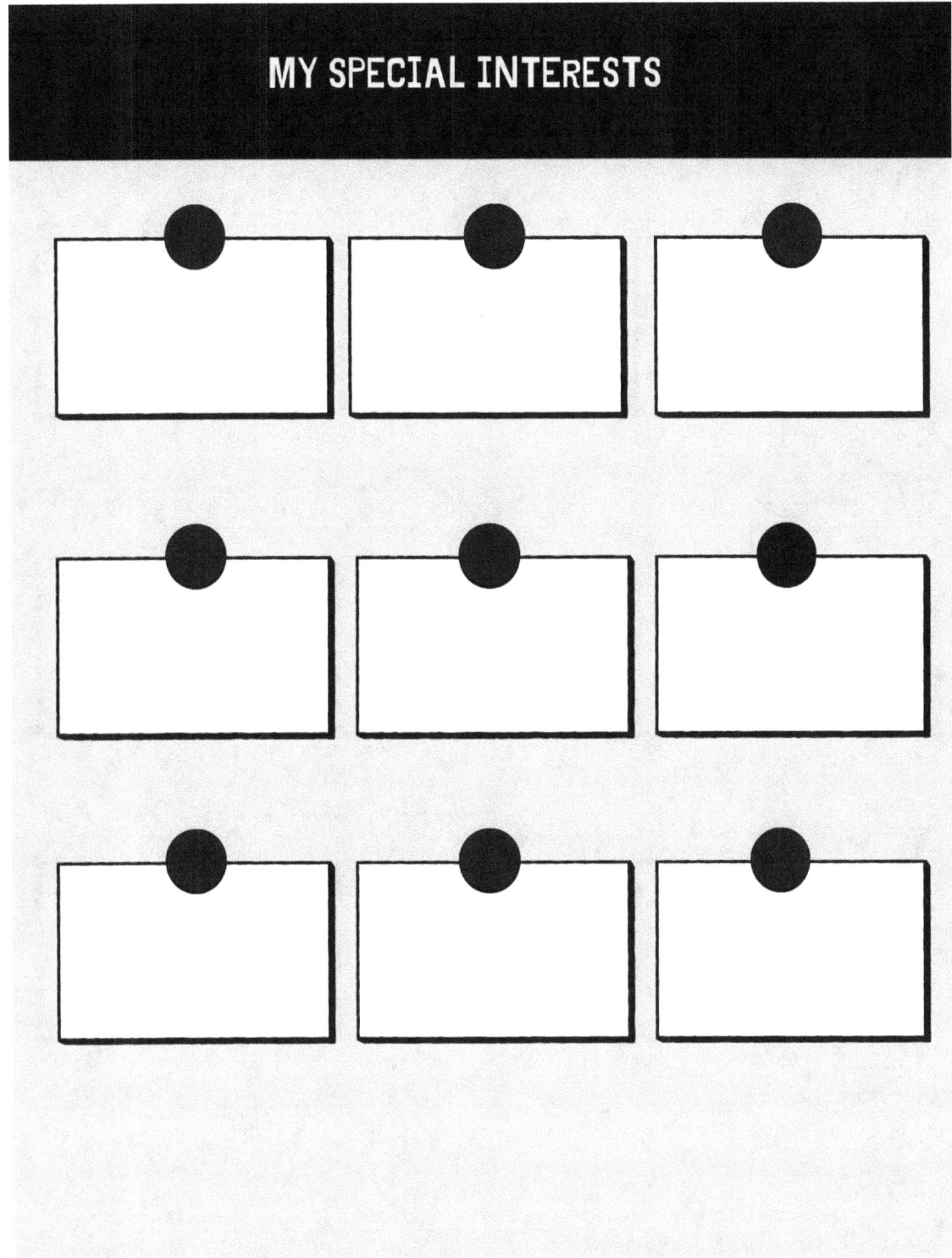

Blank Special Interests form

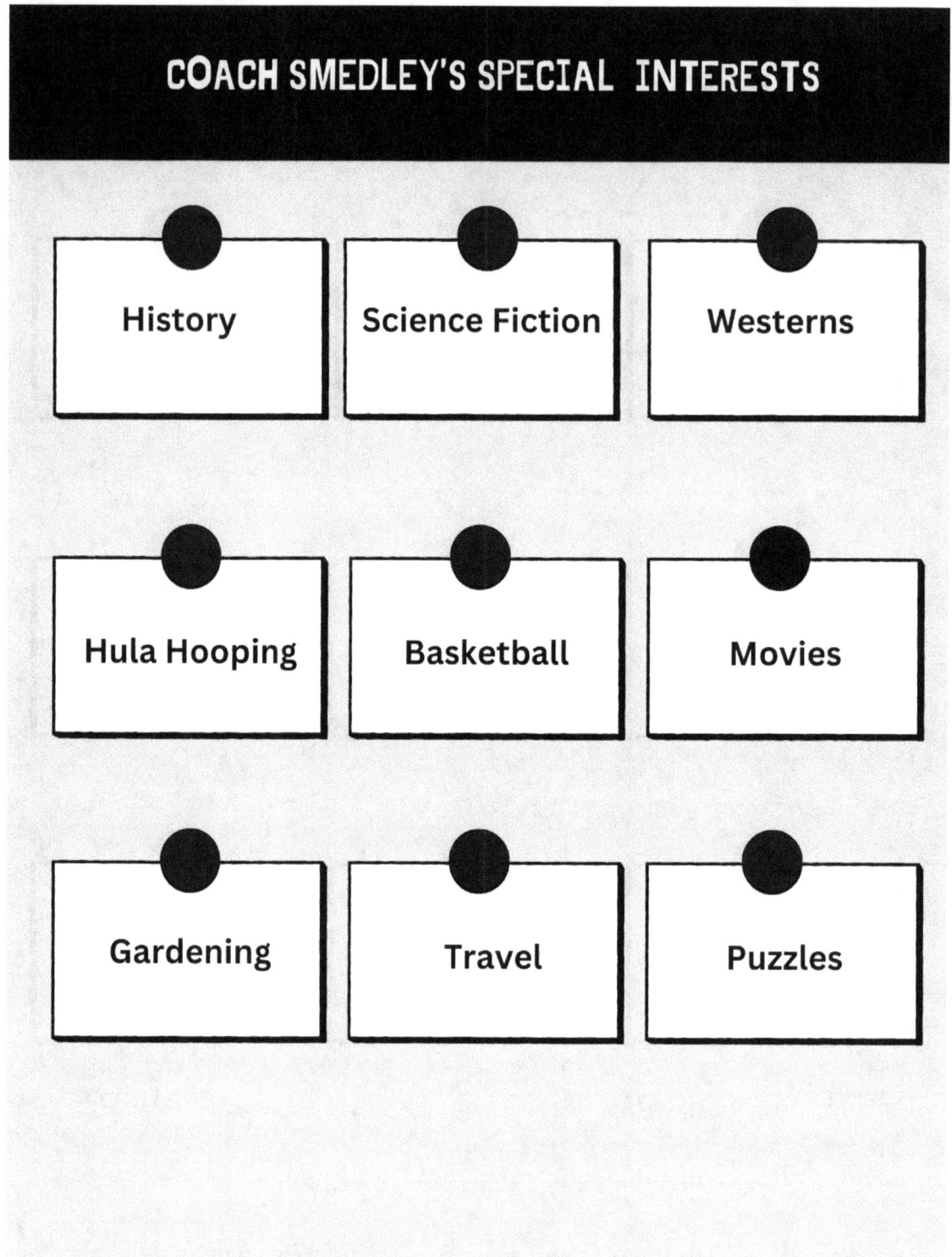

Coach Smedley's Special Interests form

Voices from the Field

When I worked at a correctional facility outside of Washington, DC, a retired scientist named Andrew contacted me and asked to volunteer with incarcerated individuals. His neighbor had volunteered with our facility for over a year and urged Andrew to call me. When I asked Andrew what he would like to share with the students he paused and replied "*I don't know.*" I found out that he retired from NASA. Andrew did not think the students would be interested in rocket science, so I asked him "*What do you love?*" Without hesitation he shared his answer. "*My bike.*" Within a month Andrew visited our classroom wearing his Tour de France biking shirt, sharing a slideshow with pictures from France, and print copies of his bike and equipment. For the next hour and a half Andrew shared his experiences with the correctional learners. They had never met a rocket scientist, or someone who ever rode in the Tour de France. As Andrew prepared to leave, he shook my hand and said "*Thank you Coach Smedley for letting an old man share his life stories. Your students were such regular people. I will never forget this experience.*" Neither would they, Andrew.

Self-Care Reminders

1. Cultivate your own special interests in a variety of areas. Do not be afraid to learn something new.

2. For added benefits, combine your special interest with social activity, academic growth, and physical movement.

3. Think back to your childhood. Recall something you have always wanted to do or learn and make it so.

My Chapter 8 Reflection

9

Lockdown

'Tis the breathing time of day with me. Williams Shakespeare

Anyone who works behind the wall will eventually experience a lockdown. Lockdown, restricted movement, lock-in, or whatever name the situation goes by in your facility means the same thing – no students. There will be times when you will be disappointed because you had big plans for the day, only to be squashed by a surprise lockdown. There will be other times when you want to jump for joy, because you need a break. I have experienced both instances.

I cannot in good conscious avoid stating an important fact about lockdowns. Something that we must remember is that lockdowns almost always have a negative effect on our students. They feel denied the opportunity to spend time in your classroom. Believe it or not, most of your students get seriously disappointed, frustrated, or even depressed when they cannot attend your class. I learned this lesson by two distinct experiences.

In the first case I had a student who I did not know very well, but his reaction to a lockdown made him unforgettable to me. We had a 3-day lockdown because of an incident in the facility. When the lockdown was lifted and classes resumed, I greeted the students back. The student I am thinking of was acting funny. He was distant. I noticed that he did not have his folder. This student took pride in having every handout, article, puzzle, etc. that I had ever passed out. He was sentenced to our jail, so he was with me for a longer stay than my typical student. The point is that he retained every single piece of paper that he had ever been given. Other students joked about how fat his folder was, and how worn it looked. That is why it was so noticeable when he did not have his folder with him. I asked him where his folder was and his response shocked me. *He said he threw it away*!

When I asked this student why he would throw his folder away he said because the lockdown made him so mad that he figured what was the point. What the heck? I instantly felt two emotions. My heart broke for the student because clearly the lockdown triggered something inside of him. Simultaneously I wanted to punch him in the face for destroying MY property. I always told my students that the materials belong to me until they are released and go out and put their new skills into practice. Then the materials belong to them forever! He heard me and had gathered and kept everything I passed out.

I refrained from punching him in the face; instead I quickly turned the situation into a teachable moment. I scheduled him for office hours with me the next day. I told him not to worry, I had an idea if would trust me. When he arrived to my office hours, I handed him a brand new folder. I asked him to share what he was feeling. I listened attentively and offered some feedback. I explained that life will be filled with disappointment. The lockdown would not be the last time that he would feel disappointment. I went on to say that after the lockdown passed here we are still in class! Life goes on. He shared that he thought I would be mad at him and worried about being kicked out of the program. We spent the remainder of the office hours "recreating" his folder. I went through my Magic File Cabinet and pulled out months' worth of handouts. I told him that he had just learned a valuable lesson about handling disappointment. You do not react in ways that only hurt you. We must be more mature than that. I ended this teachable moment with a threat to punch him in the face if he threw another one of my folders away!

The second student that comes to mind took a more radical approach during a lockdown. In his case, the facility went on lockdown in the afternoon due to a mechanical issue in the building. Just as a precaution the Warden shut everything down while repairs were being made. This second student did not know the reason for the lockdown (students often don't know why a lockdown is called until later). Well after the lockdown was lifted the next morning we returned to normal scheduling. This student filed a grievance stating that officers were purposely keeping him from class the day before. He noted the names of the officers on duty, and even added my name to the form. I was notified when the Shift Commander called me to his office and showed me the grievance form. He smiled and asked my secret to engaging this student. The young man was actually a known troublemaker who had been kicked out of other programs in the building. Here he was filing a grievance because he thought there was a conspiracy to keep him away from his education. We have the best job in the world, don't we?

THE MAIN POINT

Lockdowns have an invisible effect on everyone in the building. Officers may have heightened anxiety, and inmates can experience helplessness and isolation. Be aware of the effect of a lockdown on you and have a plan for self-care.

MY "AHA" MOMENT

Early in my career I experienced my first lockdown. I had a co-worker who was full of glee. I mean literally bouncing around, going to hang out in other people's offices, living his best life. Me on the other hand, found myself sad that my lesson plan would go to waste. I also felt bad for my students who would be in their cells all day. When very serious incidents happened, they were in total lock down and would even have to eat meals in their cells. To cope with this roller coaster of emotion, I began keeping a lockdown folder.

As I would run across interesting articles in journals, or magazines I would save them for lockdown days when I had extra time. I also bookmarked webinars or short training videos. In other words, lockdowns for me became a time to learn something new, reset my focus, and revive my creative energy. I created new classroom activities during lockdowns. I cleaned my desk or my desktop on the computer. When you find yourself in the middle of a lockdown, work on yourself or work on creating something new for your students. You will be glad that you used the time wisely.

Professional Development Activity

It is very helpful to have some small projects in mind prior to a lockdown. I keep a list of 15 minutes or less projects, 1 hour projects, or 2 hour projects nearby in case I find some extra time. The form below may help you think about tasks before the next lockdown.

Things to Do During a Lockdown

☐

☐

☐

☐

☐

☐

☐

☐

☐

☐

☐

☐

Things to Do During a Lockdown form

Voices from the Field

Angel from New Jersey shared with me that during lockdowns, "*I always have packet work ready. Also, my students can send me messages on the Kiosk to request specific materials. I have a basket in the Shift Commander's office to make it easy for the officers to return any materials to me.*" Stacey from Iowa uses the time to "*do research. I look up anything related to school. I love easy games that I can turn into classroom games. One time I spent a lockdown making a Jeopardy board. I also check with peers to see what activities they have done with success.*"

Self-Care Reminders

1. Save interesting websites, videos, or articles for those moments when you have quiet time to spare.

2. Create a success album (either digital or hard copy) where you gather your accomplishments. It is a good reminder to celebrate yourself every now and then.

3. Read a good book.

My Chapter 9 Reflection

10

The Next Generation

In each of us are places where we have never gone. Only by pressing the limits do you ever find them. Joyce Brothers

You made it to Chapter 10. I hope you have come to realize just how magical our jobs are! Think about it. We meet our students at one of the lowest points in their lives. We walk with them for months, or years while helping them to discover themselves. I have looked into many vulnerable eyes asking *"Coach Smedley do you really think I can do it?"* And that's when I respond *"Yes, I do!"* enthusiastically. Wow! Playing a part in building someone's confidence is no small feat. I tell students that I will believe in you until you can believe in yourself.

The correctional educator has an opportunity to help our learners to reinvent themselves. We often take students who never liked school and turn them into scholars. It takes a very special person to do this year after year...in a correctional setting. Many teachers will leave the field because we have such a tough job. Working conditions, safety concerns, and lack of support causes high turnover in many regions. We must support and protect the next generation of teachers!

How many times has valuable institutional knowledge been lost when a key staff person leaves the organization? I have seen this happen many times in the correctional setting. The new teacher will often have to start from scratch in their program. Does this sound familiar to anyone?

THE MAIN POINT

Every year in the correctional education space we lose experienced teachers. We need to retain the specialized knowledge and skills that will keep teachers safe and effective. Challenge yourself into capturing and sharing your lessons learned in a meaningful way.

MY "AHA" MOMENT

I realized that I was a role model for other teachers a few years ago. A new teacher who I did not know well came into my classroom one day. She walked in and looked around suspiciously, trying to see if we were alone. Once she was confident that no one else was around she quietly asked if she could talk to me. Her exact words were "*I don't know if I can trust you, but I see that you don't gossip like others around here*," she said. I smiled and asked her what was on her mind.

This teacher shared her concerns and told me how she was feeling at the time after being on the job for about six months. I patiently listened and when she was done, I assured her that she was not crazy! I had worked in this same toxic environment for 5 years and I knew exactly what she was talking about. I offered wisdom about how to navigate those shark infested waters.

Sometimes helping the next generation involves class-room tips. Other times it means providing survival strate-gies for a what can be a tough work environment. I was honored that this teacher noticed how I carried myself at all times. I interacted with staff, inmates, community partners and anyone else I encountered in the same way. I was professional, mature, and focused on doing the job to the best of my ability. My no-nonsense manner became a stabilizing force in our department. Like an anchor that is not uprooted by the tossing of the waves, I was a steady and constant presence. I could be counted on to do the right thing, to tell the truth, to own my mistakes, and to get things done.

In a nutshell, that approach is how Coach Smedley has survived (and thrived) in correctional education. At this point in my career, I concentrate on preparing the next generation of teachers. I hope that some of you will consider joining this elite club of competent, seasoned professionals.

The fact that you are still working in the trenches is a badge of honor. After surviving years in the correctional classroom, you have learned a thing or two. Think about ways that you can teach other teachers, either formally or informally. You can start by creating presentations or activity handouts highlighting your greatest hits. When you have two or three original presentations, think about submitting to present at a local or national conference. That may sound scary to you but remember there is some struggling teacher out there who needs you.

Here are three reasons to take your classroom show on the road:

- ### Mastering Your Topic

Teaching others requires you to become good at explaining the fundamentals. You will organize your topic, identify your learning objectives, and outline the content. Sharing this knowledge with your peers prepares the next generation in practical ways.

- ### Building a Professional Network

As you share your best practices, war stories, and advice you can begin to build a vast professional network. Conferences are a wonderful place to network and spend time with others who understand your work. I suggest that you strategically look for people from your state, neighboring states and across the country. You can gain knowledge of how different states handle similar challenges.

- ### Improving Correctional Education

Correctional education has not always received the respect it deserves. In some situations facilities lack innovation in the classroom. Your contribution can literally improve the whole industry and indirectly benefit the lives of the incarcerated person. This is the far-reaching gift that changes the culture of Corrections. The focus of Corrections fluctuates between punishment, rehabilitation, and restoration. Politics aside, Our nation locks up a lot of people. We must find ways to help those who will come back into our communities. Hopefully as a whole person. Correctional educators play an important role in making successful re-entry happen.

Professional Development Activity

For our final professional development activity, I would like for you to review the work you have done throughout the guide. After reviewing your notes, please reflect on your current situation on the job. Where are you? Where are you heading on this current course? Has **Practical Topics in Correctional Education Vol. 1** helped you? Write your responses on a blank sheet of paper.

Voices from the Field

The last voice from the field will be my mentee, Travis from South Carolina. As a justice involved educator Travis dreamed of presenting at a national conference. In the year that I have coached Travis, he watched me prepare to travel across the country for various events. Finally, in late 2022 I invited Travis to co-present with me on a virtual conference. We developed the content, rehearsed our presentation and ultimately held a workshop with over 180 attendees. A week after our presentation, Travis posted on social media *"I would have gone another year before fulfilling my dream of becoming a conference presenter. Thanks to a 'shove' from Coach Smedley, I can cross that goal off of my bucket list."* Someone needs what you have and what you know. Go out there and shine.

Self-Care Reminders

1. Take time to review your career (and your life). Are you where you want to be? Take a proactive step

before you react to stressors.

2. Review your life satisfaction in areas outside of your career. What's working? What's not? Is your life in balance?

3. Get your annual check-ups. You must take care of your body.

My Chapter 10 Reflection

Conclusion

T hank you for sharing this journey with me. I hope that you found something useful within these pages. Coach Smedley plans to continue sharing other nuggets of wisdom on correctional education. Now that we have taken a road trip together, I would like to invite you to submit thoughts, comments, or stories for future publications like this. Or maybe you would like information about getting your experiences in a book. I would be happy to help with that, too.

Before we end, I invite you to go back and take a look at the quotes at the beginning of each chapter. Quotes are a strategy that I use in my classroom. I give quotes to my students, only I call them **vitamins**. Vitamins are supplements that give you nutrients that you may be missing. Incarceration can be such a negative environment that I began giving my students a little square sheet of paper with a new quote each week. These quotes introduced students to philosophers from Socrates to Dr. Seuss. Now you have ten quotes to start your collection.

Coach Smedley is available if you need resources or moral support. My contact information can be found on the About the Author page. You can also find other books by me at the back of the book.

Safe travels!

– Coach Smedley

Additional Questions

If this guide has sparked additional questions, feel free to send them to Coach Smedley. All correspondence can be sent to:

Coach Smedley, 1971 Western Avenue, #238, Albany, NY 12203. Or emailed to beinspired@coachsmedley.com

About the Author

Coach Alisa Smedley has over twenty years of correctional education experience. Her unique perspective stems from personal and professional experiences in the field. The child of an incarcerated parent, Coach Smedley has deeply personal insight about the effect of incarceration on family members. Her work at a maximum security correctional facility for ten years highlighted her remarkable student engagement skills.

Coach Smedley currently travels the country providing professional development training to re-entry programs. Coach Smedley seeks to maximize safety, increase effectiveness, and extend the "shelf-life" of correctional professionals. Her strong belief is that well trained individual classroom teachers hold the power to inspire correctional learners toward successful re-entry. Her mission is to equip correctional educators with the tools to do the job with excellence.

Alisa lives in New York. Her interests include military history, reading, and travelling to new places.

Contact Information: 1971 Western Avenue, #238, Albany, NY 12203 / (202) 630-8383 / beinspired@coachsmedley.com

Also By Alisa Smedley

Practical Topics in Correctional Education Vol. II

Vitamins: 100 Powerful Quotes for the Correctional Classroom

Movies with a Message: Guide for Correctional Classrooms

Embracing Your Story: How to Build a Great Life Out of Hardships

www.ingramcontent.com/pod-product-compliance
Lightning Source LLC
Chambersburg PA
CBHW081002140626
46546CB00018B/2953